© 2024 by FAISAL JAMIL. All rights reserved.

Title: "Insightful Minds: Mastering Analytical Thinking and Innovation"

This book, along with its contents encompassing text, illustrations, images, diagrams, and other creative elements, is the exclusive property of FAISAL JAMIL and is safeguarded by copyright law.

FAISAL JAMIL asserts full ownership and retains all rights to this book. No part of this publication may be reproduced, distributed, or transmitted in any form or by any means, such as photocopying, recording, or electronic methods, without prior written consent from the copyright holder. Brief quotations in critical reviews and certain noncommercial uses permitted by copyright law are exceptions.

This copyright notice applies to all editions, formats, and translations of the book, whether in print, digital, or any other medium or technology existing now or developed in the future. Unauthorized use or infringement may result in legal action and pursuit of remedies under applicable copyright laws.

While efforts have been made to ensure accuracy and reliability, FAISAL JAMIL does not guarantee the completeness or suitability of the information. Readers are responsible for evaluating and using the content judiciously.

FAISAL JAMIL reserves the right to make changes, updates, or corrections to the book without prior notice. Inclusion of third-party materials or references does not imply endorsement or affiliation unless used under fair use principles or with proper permissions and attributions.

For permissions, inquiries, or requests regarding the book's use, please contact FAISAL JAMIL through official channels listed on their Amazon author page or provided email address.

This comprehensive copyright notice serves to protect FAISAL JAMIL'S intellectual property rights, maintain content control, and inform users about associated restrictions and permissions.

Warm regards,

FAISAL JAMIL

For your feedback and reviews:

http://www.amazon.com/author/faisal.jamil

Email: faisaljamilauthor@gmail.com

About the author

Certainly! Faisal Jamil is a multifaceted individual with a diverse set of skills and experiences. With a strong foundation in computer knowledge since childhood, he has developed a deep understanding of technology that informs his work as a content writer. Faisal also possesses digital skills, which further enhance his abilities in various digital platforms and technologies.

Beyond his professional endeavors, Faisal Jamil has also excelled in the martial arts, particularly Shotokan Karate, where he achieved the prestigious rank of first Dan black belt. This achievement speaks to his dedication, discipline, and commitment to personal growth and mastery.

In his professional life, Faisal Jamil has carved out a successful career in sales management within the Fast Moving Consumer Goods (FMCG) sector. His roles in various FMCG companies have honed his skills in strategic planning, team leadership, and business development. Faisal's ability to drive sales and achieve targets has been instrumental in his career progression, showcasing his talent for identifying opportunities and delivering results.

Faisal Jamil is also deeply interested in business investment strategies, planning, and execution. His understanding of these areas has been key to his success in the business world, allowing him to make informed decisions and implement effective strategies. His ability to navigate the complexities of investment planning and execution has set him apart as a strategic thinker and a valuable asset in any business endeavor.

Overall, Faisal Jamil is a dynamic individual who combines his passion for technology, martial arts, sales management, digital skills, and business investment strategies to achieve success in diverse fields. His journey is a testament to his versatility, resilience, and continuous pursuit of excellence.

Yours Sincerely

FAISAL JAMIL

For your feedback and reviews:

https://www.amazon.com/author/faisal.jamil

Email: faisaljamilauthor@gmail.com

INSIGHTFUL MINDS MASTERING ANALYTICAL THINKING AND INNOVATION

Table of Content

Preface	7
Introduction	9
Chapter 1: The Power of Analytical Thinking	11
Chapter 2: Cultivating a Creative Mindset	23
Chapter 3: Analytical Thinking in Everyday Life	33
Chapter 4: Innovation and its Role in Progress	42
Chapter 5: The Innovation Process	52
Chapter 6: Fostering a Culture of Innovation	61
Chapter 7: Analytical Tools for Innovation	69
Chapter 8: The Future of Analytical Thinking and Innovation	83
Chapter 9: Case Studies in Analytical Thinking and Innovation	91
Chapter 10: Putting It All Together: A Roadmap to Analytical Thinking and Innovation	97
Conclusion: Embracing Analytical Thinking and Innovation for a Brighter Future	105

Preface

Welcome to "Insightful Minds: Mastering Analytical Thinking and Innovation." In today's fast-paced and ever-changing world, the ability to think analytically and innovate is more important than ever. Whether you are a business leader looking to drive innovation in your organization, a student seeking to develop your analytical thinking skills, or anyone interested in unlocking your creativity and problem-solving abilities, this book is for you.

"Insightful Minds" is a comprehensive guide that explores the principles and practices of analytical thinking and innovation. Drawing on real-world examples, practical insights, and expert advice, this book will provide you with the tools and techniques you need to succeed in today's dynamic business environment.

In the pages that follow, you will learn how to develop your analytical thinking skills, foster a culture of innovation, and drive success in both your personal and professional life. You will discover the key concepts of analytical thinking and innovation, including critical thinking, data analysis, problem-solving, creativity, and adaptability, and learn how to apply these concepts to achieve your goals.

This book is not just a theoretical exploration of analytical thinking and innovation; it is a practical guide that will help you apply these concepts in your own life. Throughout the book, you will find practical tips, personal action plans, and encouragement to help you develop your analytical thinking skills and foster innovation.

We hope that "Insightful Minds" will inspire you to think differently, challenge the status quo, and unlock your full potential. Whether you are a seasoned professional or just starting out on your journey, this book will provide you with the tools and insights you need to succeed.

Thank you for joining us on this journey of discovery. We hope that "Insightful Minds" will be a valuable resource for you as you master the art of analytical thinking and innovation.

Best regards,

FAISAL JAMIL

Introduction

In today's rapidly changing world, the ability to think analytically and innovate is more important than ever. Whether you are a business leader seeking to drive growth and competitive advantage, a student looking to enhance your problem-solving skills, or anyone interested in unlocking your creative potential, mastering analytical thinking and innovation is essential.

"Insightful Minds: Mastering Analytical Thinking and Innovation" is a comprehensive guide that explores the principles and practices of analytical thinking and innovation. Drawing on real-world examples, practical insights, and expert advice, this book will provide you with the tools and techniques you need to succeed in today's dynamic business environment.

The book is divided into several chapters, each focusing on a different aspect of analytical thinking and innovation. We will start by exploring the fundamentals of analytical thinking, including critical thinking, data analysis, and problem-solving. We will then delve into the principles of innovation, including creativity, experimentation, and adaptability.

Throughout the book, you will learn how to apply these concepts in your personal and professional life. Whether you are looking to improve your decision-making skills, develop innovative solutions to complex problems, or drive change in your organization, "Insightful Minds" will provide you with the guidance and inspiration you need to succeed.

We hope that "Insightful Minds" will inspire you to think differently, challenge the status quo, and unlock your full potential. Whether you are a seasoned professional or just starting out on your journey, this book will provide you with the tools and insights you need to succeed.

Thank you for joining us on this journey of discovery. We hope that "Insightful Minds" will be a valuable resource for you as you master the art of analytical thinking and innovation.

Best regards,

FAISAL JAMIL

Chapter 1
The Power of Analytical Thinking

A: Understanding Analytical Thinking

Analytical thinking is a cognitive process that involves breaking down complex information or problems into smaller parts to understand them better. It is a critical component of problem-solving and decision-making, allowing individuals to analyze situations, identify key issues, and develop effective solutions. In this chapter, we will delve deeper into the concept of analytical thinking, its characteristics, and its importance in various aspects of life.

1: Definition of Analytical Thinking

Analytical thinking can be defined as the ability to systematically and logically analyze information, concepts, or situations. It involves evaluating data, identifying patterns, and drawing conclusions based on evidence and reasoning. Analytical thinkers are adept at breaking down complex problems into manageable components and approaching them in a structured manner.

2: Characteristics of Analytical Thinkers

Analytical thinkers possess several key characteristics that distinguish them from others. These include:

(i): Curiosity:

Analytical thinkers are naturally curious and constantly seek to understand the underlying causes of phenomena.

(ii): Attention to Detail:

They pay close attention to detail and can spot patterns or discrepancies that others might miss.

(iii): Logical Reasoning:

They are skilled at using logic and reasoning to evaluate situations and make sound judgments.

(iv): Problem-Solving Skills:

Analytical thinkers excel at solving complex problems by breaking them down into smaller, more manageable parts.

(v): Open-Mindedness:

They are open to new ideas and perspectives, willing to consider alternative solutions to problems.

3: Importance of Analytical Thinking

Analytical thinking is crucial in various aspects of life, including:

(i): Problem-Solving:

Analytical thinking is essential for identifying and solving problems effectively. By breaking down complex issues into smaller parts, individuals can develop targeted solutions.

(ii): Decision-Making:

Analytical thinking helps individuals make informed decisions by analyzing data, weighing options, and considering potential outcomes.

(iii): Critical Thinking:

Analytical thinking is a key component of critical thinking, which involves evaluating information and arguments to make reasoned judgments.

(iv): Innovation:

Analytical thinking is fundamental to innovation, as it enables individuals to identify new opportunities, challenge assumptions, and develop innovative solutions.

4: Developing Analytical Thinking Skills

While some individuals may naturally possess strong analytical thinking skills, others can develop these skills through practice and effort. Some strategies for developing analytical thinking skills include:

Practice solving puzzles and brainteasers to enhance problem-solving abilities.

Engage in activities that require logical reasoning, such as playing strategy games or learning a new programming language.

Analyze case studies or real-world scenarios to improve analytical thinking abilities.

Seek feedback from others to gain new perspectives and refine analytical thinking skills.

In conclusion, analytical thinking is a valuable skill that plays a vital role in problem-solving, decision-making, and innovation. By understanding the principles of analytical thinking and practicing its techniques, individuals can enhance their ability to analyze information effectively and make sound judgments in various aspects of life.

B: Importance in Problem-Solving

Analytical thinking is a critical component of effective problem-solving. It involves the ability to analyze complex situations, identify key issues, and develop practical solutions. In this chapter, we will explore the significance of analytical thinking in problem-solving and how it can lead to more effective and efficient outcomes.

1: Understanding Problem-Solving

Problem-solving is the process of identifying problems, developing solutions, and implementing them to achieve a desired outcome. It involves several steps, including defining the problem, generating possible solutions, evaluating those solutions, and implementing the best one. Effective problem-solving requires critical thinking, creativity, and analytical thinking skills.

2: Role of Analytical Thinking in Problem-Solving

Analytical thinking plays a crucial role in problem-solving in the following ways:

(i): Identifying the Problem:

Analytical thinking helps in identifying the root cause of a problem by analyzing the underlying issues and factors contributing to it.

(ii): Generating Solutions:

Analytical thinkers can generate a wide range of possible solutions by breaking down the problem into smaller, more manageable parts and exploring different approaches.

(iii): Evaluating Solutions:

Analytical thinking enables individuals to evaluate potential solutions based on their feasibility, effectiveness, and potential impact.

(iv): Selecting the Best Solution:

Analytical thinking helps in selecting the best solution by weighing the pros and cons of each option and choosing the one that is most likely to achieve the desired outcome.

(v): Implementing the Solution:

Analytical thinking also plays a role in implementing the chosen solution by developing an action plan, identifying resources needed, and monitoring progress.

3: Benefits of Analytical Thinking in Problem-Solving

The use of analytical thinking in problem-solving offers several benefits:

(i): Efficiency:

Analytical thinking can lead to more efficient problem-solving by helping individuals focus on the most critical aspects of a problem and develop targeted solutions.

(ii): Accuracy:

Analytical thinking can improve the accuracy of problem-solving by ensuring that solutions are based on evidence and logical reasoning rather than assumptions or guesswork.

(iii): Innovation:

Analytical thinking can lead to innovative solutions by encouraging individuals to think outside the box and consider alternative approaches to a problem.

(iv): Confidence:

Analytical thinking can boost confidence in problem-solving by providing a structured approach that increases the likelihood of success.

4: Developing Analytical Thinking for Problem-Solving

Developing strong analytical thinking skills can enhance problem-solving abilities. Some strategies for developing analytical thinking skills include:

(i): Practice:

Engage in activities that require analytical thinking, such as solving puzzles, analyzing data, or evaluating arguments.

(ii): Seek Feedback:

Seek feedback from others to gain new perspectives and insights that can help improve analytical thinking skills.

(iii): Think Critically:

Engage in critical thinking by questioning assumptions, evaluating evidence, and considering alternative viewpoints.

(iv): Use Analytical Tools:

Use analytical tools and techniques, such as SWOT analysis or decision matrices, to structure your thinking and approach to problem-solving.

In conclusion, analytical thinking is a crucial skill in problem-solving that can lead to more effective and efficient outcomes. By understanding the role of analytical thinking in problem-solving and practicing its techniques, individuals can enhance their problem-solving abilities and achieve better results in various aspects of life.

C: Developing Analytical Skills

Analytical skills are essential for effective problem-solving, decision-making, and critical thinking. They involve the ability to gather, analyze, and interpret information to understand complex problems and develop solutions. In this chapter, we will explore strategies for developing and improving analytical skills.

1: What Are Analytical Skills?

Analytical skills refer to the ability to collect and analyze information, problem-solve, and make decisions. These skills include:

(i): Critical Thinking:

Analyzing information objectively and evaluating arguments to make reasoned judgments.

(ii): Data Analysis:

Interpreting data and identifying trends or patterns to draw conclusions.

(iii): Research Skills:

Gathering information from various sources and evaluating its relevance and reliability.

(iv): Problem-Solving:

Identifying problems, generating solutions, and implementing them effectively.

(v): Decision-Making:

Evaluating options and making informed decisions based on available information.

2: Why Are Analytical Skills Important?

Analytical skills are crucial in various aspects of life, including:

(i): Work:

Analytical skills are highly valued by employers as they are essential for problem-solving, decision-making, and innovation.

(ii): Education:

Analytical skills are essential for academic success, including analyzing texts, solving mathematical problems, and conducting research.

(iii): Everyday Life:

Analytical skills help in making informed decisions, solving problems, and understanding complex issues in daily life.

3: Strategies for Developing Analytical Skills

There are several strategies you can use to develop and improve your analytical skills:

(i): Practice Critical Thinking:

Engage in activities that require critical thinking, such as solving puzzles, analyzing arguments, or evaluating evidence.

(ii): Read Widely:

Reading a variety of materials can expose you to different perspectives and help you develop a more analytical mindset.

(iii): Develop Research Skills:

Practice gathering information from various sources, evaluating its credibility, and synthesizing it to draw conclusions.

(iv): Solve Problems:

Engage in problem-solving activities, such as solving riddles or puzzles, to sharpen your analytical skills.

(v): Seek Feedback:

Seek feedback from others to gain new perspectives and insights that can help you improve your analytical skills.

4: Applying Analytical Skills

Once you have developed your analytical skills, you can apply them in various ways, including:

(i): Problem-Solving:

Use your analytical skills to identify problems, analyze them, and develop effective solutions.

(ii): Decision-Making:

Use analytical thinking to evaluate options and make informed decisions based on available information.

(iii): Critical Thinking:

Apply critical thinking skills to analyze information, evaluate arguments, and make reasoned judgments.

(iv): Research:

Use your research skills to gather information, analyze data, and draw conclusions in academic or professional settings.

In conclusion, developing analytical skills is essential for success in work, education, and everyday life. By practicing critical thinking, improving research skills, and applying analytical thinking in various situations, you can enhance your analytical skills and achieve better outcomes in all aspects of life.

Chapter 2
Cultivating a Creative Mindset

A: The Relationship Between Analytical Thinking and Creativity

Analytical thinking and creativity are often seen as two distinct cognitive processes, with analytical thinking being associated with logic and reasoning, and creativity being associated with imagination and innovation. However, these two processes are closely intertwined and often complement each other. In this chapter, we will explore the relationship between analytical thinking and creativity and how they can work together to enhance problem-solving and innovation.

1: Understanding Analytical Thinking and Creativity

Analytical thinking is the process of breaking down complex information into smaller, more manageable parts to understand it better. It involves logical reasoning, critical thinking, and a systematic approach to problem-solving. Creativity, on the other hand, is the ability to generate new ideas, concepts, or solutions that are original and valuable. It involves thinking outside the box, exploring new possibilities, and making connections between seemingly unrelated ideas.

2: The Role of Analytical Thinking in Creativity

While creativity is often associated with "thinking outside the box," analytical thinking plays a crucial role in this process. Analytical thinking helps to:

(i): Define the Problem:

Analytical thinking can help to define the problem more clearly by breaking it down into its fundamental components and understanding the underlying issues.

(ii): Generate Ideas:

Analytical thinking can generate a wide range of ideas by exploring different perspectives and approaches to the problem.

(iii): Evaluate Ideas:

Analytical thinking can evaluate the feasibility and effectiveness of ideas by considering their practicality and potential impact.

(iv): Refine Ideas:

Analytical thinking can refine and improve ideas by identifying strengths and weaknesses and making necessary adjustments.

3: The Role of Creativity in Analytical Thinking

Creativity also plays a vital role in analytical thinking by:

(i): Generating Solutions:

Creativity can generate innovative solutions to problems that may not be apparent through traditional analytical methods.

(ii): Breaking Mental Blocks:

Creativity can help break through mental blocks or fixed patterns of thinking that may hinder analytical thinking.

(iii): Encouraging Exploration:

Creativity encourages exploration and experimentation, leading to new insights and discoveries in the analytical process.

4: Enhancing Analytical Thinking and Creativity

To enhance both analytical thinking and creativity, individuals can:

(i): Practice Divergent Thinking:

Divergent thinking is the ability to generate a variety of ideas or solutions to a problem. Practicing divergent thinking can enhance creativity.

(ii): Seek Novelty:

Exposing oneself to new experiences, ideas, and perspectives can stimulate creativity and enhance analytical thinking.

(iii): Combine Analytical and Creative Processes:

Combining analytical thinking with creative thinking can lead to innovative solutions that are both practical and original.

5: Conclusion

In conclusion, analytical thinking and creativity are not mutually exclusive but are instead complementary processes that can enhance problem-solving and innovation. By understanding the relationship between these two processes and practicing techniques to enhance both, individuals can become more effective problem solvers and innovators in various aspects of life.

B: Techniques for Stimulating Creativity

Creativity is a valuable skill that can be developed and enhanced through various techniques and exercises. In this chapter, we will explore some effective techniques for stimulating creativity and generating new ideas.

1: Brainstorming

Brainstorming is a popular technique for generating ideas in a group setting. It involves gathering a group of people and encouraging them to come up with as many ideas as possible, no matter how wild or impractical. The goal is to generate a large quantity of ideas, which can then be evaluated and refined later.

2: Mind Mapping

Mind mapping is a visual technique for organizing thoughts and ideas. It involves creating a diagram that starts with a central idea and branches out into related ideas and concepts. Mind mapping can help stimulate creativity by allowing you to see connections between different ideas and explore new possibilities.

3: Role Playing

Role playing involves taking on different perspectives or personas to generate new ideas. By imagining yourself in someone else's shoes, you can gain new insights and think about problems or situations in a different way. Role playing can help break out of fixed patterns of thinking and stimulate creativity.

4: Free Writing

Free writing is a technique where you write continuously for a set period of time without worrying about grammar, spelling, or coherence. The goal is to get your ideas down on paper without censoring yourself. Free writing can help stimulate creativity by allowing you to explore ideas freely and without constraints.

5: Mindfulness and Meditation

Mindfulness and meditation techniques can help quiet the mind and enhance creativity. By practicing mindfulness, you can focus your attention and reduce mental clutter, allowing creative ideas to flow more freely. Meditation can also help you tap into your subconscious mind and access new ideas and insights.

6: Changing Your Environment

Changing your environment can help stimulate creativity by providing new stimuli and perspectives. Try working in a different location, such as a coffee shop or park, or rearranging your workspace to create a fresh and inspiring environment.

7: Collaborating with Others

Collaborating with others can stimulate creativity by exposing you to new ideas and perspectives. Working with a diverse group of people can help you see problems from different angles and generate innovative solutions.

8: Engaging in Creative Hobbies

Engaging in creative hobbies, such as painting, writing, or playing music, can help stimulate creativity in other areas of your life. These activities can help you relax, reduce stress, and tap into your creative side.

9: Conclusion

Stimulating creativity is an important skill that can help you generate new ideas, solve problems, and innovate in various aspects of your life. By practicing these techniques and incorporating them into your daily routine, you can enhance your creativity and become a more effective and innovative thinker.

C: Overcoming Creative Blocks

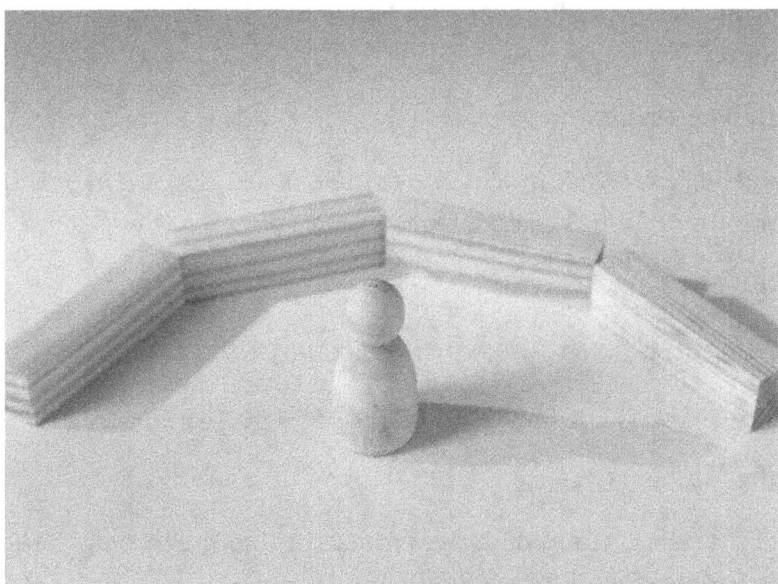

Creative blocks are common challenges that can hinder the creative process and prevent individuals from generating new ideas or solutions. In this chapter, we will explore some effective strategies for overcoming creative blocks and fostering creativity.

1: Understanding Creative Blocks

Creative blocks can manifest in various forms, such as:

(i): Lack of Inspiration:

Feeling uninspired or lacking motivation to create.

(ii): Fear of Failure:

Fear of not being able to come up with a good idea or of the idea not being well-received.

(iii): Perfectionism:

Striving for perfection and being overly critical of one's ideas.

(iv): Overwhelm:

Feeling overwhelmed by the complexity of a problem or the number of ideas to consider.

(v): Routine:

Being stuck in a routine or familiar ways of thinking.

2: Strategies for Overcoming Creative Blocks

(i): Take Breaks:

Sometimes, stepping away from a problem can help clear your mind and spark new ideas. Engage in a different activity or simply take a walk to refresh your mind.

(ii): Change Your Environment:

A change of scenery can stimulate creativity. Work in a different location or rearrange your workspace to create a new and inspiring environment.

(iii): Brainstorming:

Engage in brainstorming sessions with others to generate new ideas and perspectives. Don't judge or evaluate ideas during this process, just focus on generating as many ideas as possible.

(iv): Mindfulness and Meditation:

Practice mindfulness or meditation to quiet your mind and reduce stress, which can help enhance creativity.

(v): Creative Exercises:

Engage in creative exercises or activities, such as drawing, writing, or playing music, to stimulate your creativity and get your creative juices flowing.

(vi): Limitations:

Sometimes, imposing limitations or constraints on your creative process can actually enhance creativity. For example, give yourself a time limit or work within a specific theme.

(vii): Seek Inspiration:

Look for inspiration in books, art, nature, or other sources. Exposing yourself to new ideas and perspectives can help stimulate your own creativity.

(viii): Relaxation Techniques:

Engage in relaxation techniques, such as deep breathing or progressive muscle relaxation, to reduce stress and anxiety that may be inhibiting your creativity.

(ix): Seek Feedback:

Share your ideas with others and seek feedback. Sometimes, a fresh perspective can help you see your ideas in a new light and overcome creative blocks.

3: Conclusion

Creative blocks are a common challenge, but they can be overcome with the right strategies and techniques. By understanding the causes of creative blocks and implementing strategies to overcome them, you can foster creativity and continue to generate new ideas and solutions.

Chapter 3
Analytical Thinking in Everyday Life

A: Applying Analytical Thinking in Personal and Professional Settings

Analytical thinking is a valuable skill that can be applied in various personal and professional settings to enhance decision-making, problem-solving, and critical thinking. In this chapter, we will explore how analytical thinking can be applied in different contexts to achieve better outcomes.

1: Personal Finance

In personal finance, analytical thinking can help individuals make informed decisions about budgeting, investing, and saving. By analyzing their income, expenses, and financial goals, individuals can develop a financial plan that aligns with their objectives and helps them achieve financial stability.

2: Time Management

Analytical thinking can also be applied to time management. By analyzing how time is currently being spent and identifying areas where time could be better allocated, individuals can optimize their schedules and improve productivity.

3: Problem-Solving

Analytical thinking is fundamental to problem-solving in both personal and professional settings. By breaking down complex problems into smaller, more manageable parts, individuals can identify root causes and develop effective solutions.

4: Critical Thinking

Analytical thinking is closely related to critical thinking, which involves evaluating information and arguments to make reasoned judgments. In personal and professional settings, critical thinking can help individuals assess the validity of information and make informed decisions.

5: Decision-Making

Analytical thinking is essential for effective decision-making. By analyzing relevant information, considering alternative options, and evaluating potential outcomes, individuals can make decisions that are well-informed and likely to lead to positive results.

6: Project Management

In project management, analytical thinking is crucial for planning, executing, and monitoring projects. By analyzing project requirements, identifying potential risks, and developing contingency plans, project managers can ensure that projects are completed successfully and on time.

7: Conclusion

In conclusion, analytical thinking is a valuable skill that can be applied in various personal and professional settings to enhance decision-making, problem-solving, and critical thinking. By developing and honing their analytical thinking skills, individuals can improve their ability to analyze information, make informed decisions, and achieve better outcomes in all aspects of their lives.

B: Examples of Analytical Thinking in Action

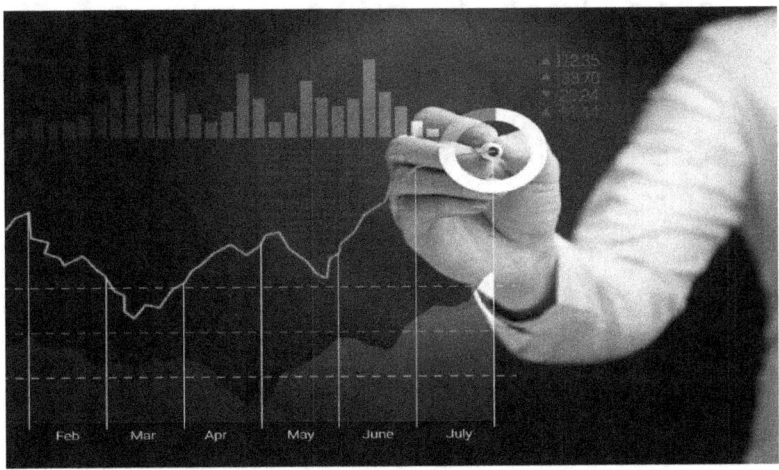

Analytical thinking is a valuable skill that can be applied in a wide range of situations. In this chapter, we will explore some examples of analytical thinking in action to illustrate how it can be used to solve problems, make decisions, and achieve better outcomes.

1: Example 1: Business Strategy

In a business setting, analytical thinking is essential for developing and implementing effective strategies. For example, a company may use analytical thinking to analyze market trends, competitor strategies, and customer preferences to develop a strategic plan that aligns with its goals and objectives.

2: Example 2: Data Analysis

Analytical thinking is also crucial for data analysis. For example, a data analyst may use analytical thinking to analyze large datasets, identify patterns and trends, and draw conclusions that can inform business decisions.

3: Example 3: Problem-Solving

Analytical thinking is fundamental to problem-solving. For example, a project manager faced with a project delay may use analytical thinking to identify the root cause of the delay, develop a plan to address it, and implement solutions to ensure the project stays on track.

4: Example 4: Critical Thinking

Analytical thinking is closely related to critical thinking, which involves evaluating information and arguments to make reasoned judgments. For example, a manager may use critical thinking to assess the validity of a new business proposal and make a decision on whether to pursue it.

5: Example 5: Decision-Making

Analytical thinking is essential for effective decision-making. For example, a financial analyst may use analytical thinking to analyze investment options, evaluate risks and returns, and make recommendations on where to allocate funds.

6: Example 6: Academic Research

In academic research, analytical thinking is crucial for analyzing data, developing hypotheses, and drawing conclusions. For example, a researcher may use analytical thinking to analyze the results of a study and draw conclusions that contribute to the body of knowledge in their field.

7: Conclusion

These examples illustrate the diverse applications of analytical thinking in various settings. By developing and honing their analytical thinking skills, individuals can improve their ability to solve problems, make informed decisions, and achieve better outcomes in both their personal and professional lives.

C: Improving Decision-Making Through Analysis

Analytical thinking plays a crucial role in improving decision-making by enabling individuals to analyze information, evaluate options, and make informed choices. In this chapter, we will explore how analysis can enhance decision-making in both personal and professional contexts.

1: Understanding Decision-Making

Decision-making is the process of selecting the best course of action from among multiple options. It involves gathering information, analyzing it, and evaluating the possible outcomes of each option before making a choice.

2: The Role of Analysis in Decision-Making

Analysis is essential for effective decision-making as it allows individuals to:

(i): Gather Information:

Analysis helps in collecting relevant data and information needed to make a decision.

(ii): Evaluate Options:

Analysis enables individuals to evaluate the pros and cons of each option and assess their potential impact.

(iii): Predict Outcomes:

Analysis helps in predicting the likely outcomes of each option based on available information and past experiences.

(iv): Make Informed Choices:

Analysis provides a structured approach to decision-making, allowing individuals to make informed choices that are based on evidence and reasoning.

3: Techniques for Improving Decision-Making Through Analysis

Some techniques for improving decision-making through analysis include:

(i): SWOT Analysis:

SWOT analysis is a strategic planning tool that helps in identifying strengths, weaknesses, opportunities, and threats related to a decision. It can help in evaluating the internal and external factors that may impact a decision.

(ii): Cost-Benefit Analysis:

Cost-benefit analysis involves comparing the costs of a decision with its benefits to determine whether the benefits outweigh the costs. It can help in assessing the financial viability of a decision.

(iii): Risk Analysis:

Risk analysis involves identifying potential risks associated with a decision and assessing their likelihood and impact. It can help in mitigating risks and making more informed decisions.

(iv): Decision Trees:

Decision trees are graphical representations of decisions and their potential outcomes. They can help in visualizing different decision paths and their consequences, making it easier to choose the best course of action.

4: Applying Analysis in Personal Decision-Making

In personal decision-making, analysis can help in:

(i): Career Planning:

Analyzing career options, evaluating job offers, and making informed decisions about career paths.

(ii): Financial Planning:

Analyzing financial goals, evaluating investment options, and making informed decisions about saving and investing.

(iii): Healthcare Decisions:

Analyzing healthcare options, evaluating treatment plans, and making informed decisions about medical care.

5: Applying Analysis in Professional Decision-Making

In professional decision-making, analysis can help in:

(i): Strategic Planning:

Analyzing market trends, evaluating competitor strategies, and making informed decisions about business strategies.

(ii): Project Management:

Analyzing project requirements, evaluating risks, and making informed decisions about project plans.

(iii): Human Resource Management:

Analyzing workforce needs, evaluating candidates, and making informed decisions about hiring and staffing.

6: Conclusion

Analysis is a powerful tool for improving decision-making in both personal and professional settings. By applying analytical thinking and techniques, individuals can gather information, evaluate options, and make informed choices that lead to better outcomes.

Chapter 4
Innovation and its Role in Progress

A: Defining Innovation

Innovation is a multifaceted concept that encompasses the development and implementation of new ideas, processes, products, or services that create value. In this chapter, we will explore the various aspects of innovation and how it contributes to progress and growth in different fields.

1: Understanding Innovation

At its core, innovation involves the creation and implementation of new ideas or concepts that lead to significant change or improvement. It is not limited to the invention of new products or technologies but also includes new ways of thinking, organizing, and doing things that result in positive outcomes.

2: Types of Innovation

There are several types of innovation, including:

(i): Product Innovation:

Involves the development of new or improved products or services.

(ii): Process Innovation:

Involves the implementation of new or improved processes to increase efficiency or effectiveness.

(iii): Business Model Innovation:

Involves the creation of new business models or the modification of existing ones to create value.

(iv): Technological Innovation:

Involves the development and implementation of new technologies.

(v): Social Innovation:

Involves the development of new solutions to social or environmental challenges.

3: Characteristics of Innovation

Innovation is characterized by several key features, including:

(i): Creativity:

Innovation requires creative thinking to generate new ideas and concepts.

(ii): Risk-taking:

Innovation often involves taking risks and experimenting with new approaches.

(iii): Collaboration:

Innovation thrives in environments where there is collaboration and knowledge sharing.

(iv): Adaptability:

Innovation requires the ability to adapt to changing circumstances and incorporate feedback.

(v): Value Creation:

Innovation aims to create value for customers, organizations, or society as a whole.

4: Importance of Innovation

Innovation is essential for progress and growth in various fields, including:

(i): Economic Growth:

Innovation drives economic growth by creating new markets, increasing productivity, and fostering competition.

(ii): Competitive Advantage:

Innovation provides organizations with a competitive advantage by enabling them to differentiate themselves from competitors.

(iii): Societal Impact:

Innovation has a significant impact on society by addressing social and environmental challenges and improving quality of life.

(iv): Personal Development:

Innovation fosters personal development by encouraging individuals to think creatively, take risks, and learn from failure.

5: Innovation Process

The innovation process typically involves several stages, including:

(i): Ideation:

Generating ideas for innovation through brainstorming, research, and experimentation.

(ii): Evaluation:

Evaluating ideas based on criteria such as feasibility, viability, and potential impact.

(iii): Development:

Developing and testing prototypes or concepts to refine and improve them.

(iv): Implementation:

Implementing the innovation in the market or organization.

(v): Monitoring and Feedback:

Monitoring the performance of the innovation and gathering feedback for further improvement.

6: Conclusion

Innovation is a dynamic and essential process that drives progress and growth in various fields. By fostering a culture of innovation and embracing new ideas and concepts, individuals, organizations, and societies can achieve positive change and create a better future.

B: The Importance of Innovation in Society

Innovation plays a critical role in shaping society by driving progress, economic growth, and improvements in quality of life. In this chapter, we will explore the various ways in which innovation impacts society and why it is essential for addressing the challenges of the future.

1: Driving Economic Growth

One of the most significant impacts of innovation is its role in driving economic growth. Innovation leads to the creation of new industries, products, and services, which in turn creates jobs, increases productivity, and stimulates investment. Countries that prioritize innovation are often more competitive and resilient in the global economy.

2: Fostering Entrepreneurship

Innovation fosters entrepreneurship by providing individuals with the tools and resources they need to turn their ideas into successful businesses. Entrepreneurs drive innovation by taking risks, experimenting with new ideas, and challenging the status quo. This entrepreneurial spirit is essential for driving economic growth and creating a dynamic and competitive business environment.

3: Improving Quality of Life

Innovation has a profound impact on the quality of life by improving access to essential goods and services, such as healthcare, education, and transportation. For example, innovations in healthcare have led to significant advancements in medical treatments, disease prevention, and patient care, improving health outcomes and extending life expectancy.

4: Addressing Societal Challenges

Innovation plays a crucial role in addressing some of the most pressing societal challenges, such as poverty, hunger, and climate change. Innovations in technology, agriculture, and renewable energy are helping to create more sustainable and equitable solutions to these complex issues.

5: Stimulating Creativity and Learning

Innovation stimulates creativity and learning by encouraging individuals to think outside the box, experiment with new ideas, and embrace failure as a learning opportunity. This culture of innovation fosters a mindset of continuous learning and improvement, which is essential for personal and professional development.

6: Conclusion

Innovation is essential for driving progress and improving quality of life in society. By fostering a culture of innovation and investing in research, education, and technology, societies can create a better future for generations to come.

C: Types of Innovation

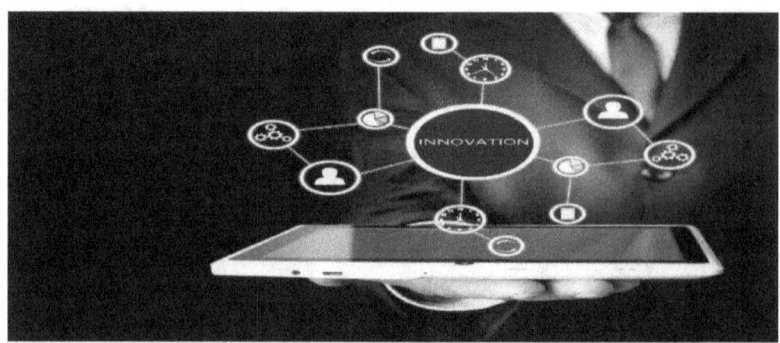

Innovation comes in various forms, each with its own unique characteristics and impact. In this chapter, we will explore the different types of innovation and how they contribute to progress and growth in different fields.

1: Product Innovation

Product innovation involves the development of new or improved products or services. This type of innovation often involves research and development (R&D) to create innovative products that meet the needs and preferences of consumers. Examples of product innovation include the development of new technologies, consumer electronics, and pharmaceuticals.

2: Process Innovation

Process innovation involves the implementation of new or improved processes to increase efficiency, reduce costs, or improve quality. This type of innovation often focuses on streamlining operations, automating tasks, or adopting new technologies to improve productivity. Examples of process innovation include lean manufacturing techniques, automation, and supply chain optimization.

3: Business Model Innovation

Business model innovation involves the creation of new business models or the modification of existing ones to create value. This type of innovation often involves rethinking how a company delivers value to customers, generates revenue, and captures market share. Examples of business model innovation include subscription-based services, freemium models, and platform-based business models.

4: Technological Innovation

Technological innovation involves the development and implementation of new technologies. This type of innovation often drives progress in various industries, such as information technology, healthcare, and transportation. Examples of technological innovation include the development of artificial intelligence, blockchain technology, and 3D printing.

5: Social Innovation

Social innovation involves the development of new solutions to social or environmental challenges. This type of innovation often focuses on creating positive social impact, such as improving access to education, healthcare, or clean energy. Examples of social innovation include microfinance, social enterprises, and community-based initiatives.

6: Sustainable Innovation

Sustainable innovation involves the development of new solutions that are environmentally sustainable. This type of innovation often focuses on reducing carbon emissions, conserving natural resources, and promoting environmental stewardship. Examples of sustainable innovation include renewable energy technologies, green building practices, and sustainable agriculture methods.

7: Conclusion

These types of innovation are not mutually exclusive and often overlap in practice. By understanding the different types of innovation and how they contribute to progress and growth, individuals, organizations, and societies can leverage innovation to create a better future for all.

Chapter 5
The Innovation Process

A: From Idea Generation to Implementation

Bringing an idea to life requires a structured approach that encompasses idea generation, development, and implementation. In this chapter, we will explore the steps involved in moving from idea generation to implementation and the key considerations at each stage.

1: Idea Generation

The first step in the innovation process is idea generation. This stage involves generating and capturing ideas that have the potential to solve a problem or meet a need. Idea generation can be facilitated through brainstorming sessions, idea competitions, or by leveraging insights from customers, employees, and other stakeholders.

2: Idea Screening and Evaluation

Once ideas have been generated, they need to be screened and evaluated to determine their feasibility and potential impact. This stage involves assessing each idea against criteria such as market demand, technical feasibility, and strategic fit. Ideas that pass this screening process move on to the next stage.

3: Concept Development

During the concept development stage, selected ideas are further refined and developed into detailed concepts. This stage involves fleshing out the idea, defining its key features and benefits, and assessing its potential market appeal. Concepts are often presented in the form of prototypes, mockups, or business plans.

4: Testing and Validation

Before moving forward with implementation, concepts need to be tested and validated to ensure that they meet the needs of the target audience. This stage involves gathering feedback from potential users, conducting market research, and refining the concept based on this feedback. Testing and validation help identify potential issues early on and mitigate risks.

5: Implementation Planning

Once a concept has been validated, the next step is to develop an implementation plan. This plan outlines the steps required to bring the idea to market, including resource allocation, timeline, and milestones. Implementation planning also involves identifying potential risks and developing contingency plans to address them.

6: Implementation and Execution

The final stage of the innovation process is implementation and execution. This stage involves putting the plan into action, launching the product or service, and monitoring its performance. Implementation requires effective project management, coordination across teams, and continuous evaluation and adjustment based on feedback.

7: Monitoring and Evaluation

After implementation, it is essential to monitor the performance of the innovation and evaluate its impact. This stage involves tracking key performance indicators (KPIs), gathering feedback from customers and stakeholders, and making adjustments as necessary to ensure the success of the innovation.

8: Conclusion

Bringing an idea to life requires a systematic approach that encompasses idea generation, development, and implementation. By following these steps and considering the key considerations at each stage, individuals, organizations, and societies can successfully move from idea generation to implementation and achieve meaningful innovation.

B: Steps in the Innovation Process

The innovation process involves a series of steps that help transform ideas into tangible products, services, or solutions. In this chapter, we will explore the key steps in the innovation process and how they contribute to the success of innovation initiatives.

Step 1: Identify Opportunities

The first step in the innovation process is to identify opportunities for innovation. This involves identifying unmet needs, emerging trends, or areas where improvements can be made. Opportunities for innovation can come from various sources, such as customer feedback, market research, or internal brainstorming sessions.

Step 2: Generate Ideas

Once opportunities have been identified, the next step is to generate ideas for innovation. This involves brainstorming and ideation sessions to come up with creative solutions to the identified opportunities. Ideas can be generated by individuals or teams and should be evaluated based on their feasibility and potential impact.

Step 3: Evaluate and Select Ideas

After ideas have been generated, they need to be evaluated and selected for further development. This involves assessing each idea against criteria such as market potential, technical feasibility, and alignment with strategic objectives. Ideas that align with the organization's goals and have the greatest potential for success are selected for further development.

Step 4: Develop Concepts

Once ideas have been selected, they are further developed into detailed concepts. This involves fleshing out the idea, defining its key features and benefits, and creating prototypes or mockups to visualize the concept. Concepts are refined based on feedback and input from stakeholders.

Step 5: Test and Validate

Before moving forward with implementation, concepts need to be tested and validated to ensure they meet the needs of the target audience. This involves conducting market research, gathering feedback from potential users, and refining the concept based on this feedback. Testing and validation help identify potential issues early on and mitigate risks.

Step 6: Develop Implementation Plan

Once a concept has been validated, an implementation plan is developed. This plan outlines the steps required to bring the idea to market, including resource allocation, timeline, and milestones. It also identifies potential risks and develops contingency plans to address them.

Step 7: Implement and Monitor

The final step in the innovation process is to implement the idea and monitor its performance. This involves putting the plan into action, launching the product or service, and monitoring its success. Monitoring involves tracking key performance indicators (KPIs), gathering feedback, and making adjustments as necessary to ensure the success of the innovation.

8: Conclusion

The innovation process is a systematic approach to transforming ideas into successful products, services, or solutions. By following these key steps and considering the needs of the target audience, organizations can increase their chances of success and drive meaningful innovation.

C: Overcoming Challenges in Innovation

Innovation is a complex process that is often fraught with challenges and obstacles. In this chapter, we will explore some of the common challenges faced by individuals and organizations in the innovation process and discuss strategies for overcoming them.

1: Lack of Resources

One of the most common challenges in innovation is a lack of resources, including financial, human, and technological resources. To overcome this challenge, organizations can seek partnerships, collaborations, and funding opportunities to support their innovation initiatives. They can also prioritize and allocate resources effectively to focus on high-potential ideas.

2: Resistance to Change

Resistance to change is another common challenge in innovation, as people may be hesitant to adopt new ideas or ways of working. To overcome this challenge, organizations can communicate the benefits of innovation, involve stakeholders in the innovation process, and provide training and support to help them adapt to change.

3: Risk Aversion

Many individuals and organizations are risk-averse, preferring to stick with what is familiar rather than taking a chance on something new. To overcome this challenge, organizations can create a culture that encourages experimentation and learning from failure. They can also implement processes for identifying and mitigating risks associated with innovation initiatives.

4: Lack of Vision or Strategy

Without a clear vision or strategy, innovation efforts can become unfocused and ineffective. To overcome this challenge, organizations can develop a clear innovation strategy that aligns with their overall goals and objectives. They can also communicate this strategy effectively to ensure that everyone is working towards the same vision.

5: Resistance to Failure

Failure is an inevitable part of the innovation process, but many individuals and organizations are resistant to it. To overcome this challenge, organizations can create a culture that embraces failure as a learning opportunity. They can encourage experimentation and provide support to help individuals learn from their mistakes.

6: Lack of Customer Understanding

Another common challenge in innovation is a lack of understanding of customer needs and preferences. To overcome this challenge, organizations can invest in market research and customer feedback mechanisms to gain insights into customer needs and preferences. They can also involve customers in the innovation process to ensure that their ideas are aligned with customer expectations.

7: Conclusion

Innovation is essential for driving progress and growth, but it is not without its challenges. By understanding and addressing these challenges, individuals and organizations can increase their chances of success and drive meaningful innovation that has a positive impact on society.

Chapter 6
Fostering a Culture of Innovation

A: Creating an Environment Conducive to Innovation

Creating an environment that fosters innovation is essential for organizations looking to drive progress and stay competitive. In this chapter, we will explore the key elements of an innovation-friendly environment and how organizations can cultivate such a culture.

1: Encouraging Creativity

One of the first steps in creating an innovation-friendly environment is to encourage creativity among employees. This can be achieved by providing opportunities for brainstorming and idea generation, as well as creating a culture that values and rewards creative thinking.

2: Promoting Collaboration

Collaboration is essential for innovation, as it allows individuals to share ideas, build on each other's strengths, and create new solutions together. Organizations can promote collaboration by creating open and flexible workspaces, encouraging cross-functional teams, and fostering a culture of knowledge sharing.

3: Embracing Diversity

Diversity of thought and perspective is crucial for innovation, as it brings together individuals with different backgrounds, experiences, and ideas. Organizations can embrace diversity by promoting inclusivity, valuing different perspectives, and creating a culture that celebrates diversity.

4: Providing Resources and Support

To foster innovation, organizations need to provide employees with the resources and support they need to explore new ideas and take risks. This can include access to training and development opportunities, funding for innovation projects, and support from leadership.

5: Empowering Employees

Empowering employees to take ownership of their ideas and initiatives is key to fostering innovation. Organizations can empower employees by giving them autonomy, providing opportunities for decision-making, and recognizing and rewarding their contributions.

6: Creating a Culture of Experimentation

Innovation often involves experimentation and taking calculated risks. Organizations can create a culture of experimentation by encouraging employees to try new things, learn from failure, and iterate on ideas to improve them.

7: Encouraging Continuous Learning

Innovation thrives in environments where learning is valued and encouraged. Organizations can promote continuous learning by providing opportunities for professional development, offering access to resources and tools, and fostering a culture of curiosity and exploration.

8: Conclusion

Creating an environment that fosters innovation requires a combination of factors, including encouraging creativity, promoting collaboration, embracing diversity, providing resources and support, empowering employees, creating a culture of experimentation, and encouraging continuous learning. By cultivating these elements, organizations can create a culture of innovation that drives progress and success.

B: Encouraging Innovation in Teams

Innovation is often a collaborative effort that involves individuals working together to generate new ideas and solutions. In this chapter, we will explore how organizations can encourage innovation in teams and harness the collective creativity and expertise of their members.

1: Building Diverse Teams

Diversity is key to innovation, as it brings together individuals with different backgrounds, experiences, and perspectives. Organizations can build diverse teams by including individuals with a range of skills, knowledge, and expertise, as well as different cultural and demographic backgrounds.

2: Fostering a Culture of Psychological Safety

Psychological safety is essential for encouraging innovation in teams, as it allows team members to feel comfortable taking risks, sharing ideas, and expressing their opinions without fear of judgment or reprisal. Organizations can foster a culture of psychological safety by promoting open communication, valuing different perspectives, and encouraging constructive feedback.

3: Providing Opportunities for Collaboration

Collaboration is essential for innovation, as it allows team members to build on each other's ideas and create new solutions together. Organizations can provide opportunities for collaboration by creating open and flexible workspaces, encouraging cross-functional teams, and facilitating knowledge sharing.

4: Encouraging Experimentation and Risk-Taking

Innovation often involves experimentation and taking calculated risks.

Organizations can encourage experimentation and risk-taking by giving teams the freedom to explore new ideas, test hypotheses, and learn from failure. This can help teams to innovate more effectively and develop new and innovative solutions.

5: Recognizing and Rewarding Innovation

Recognizing and rewarding innovation can help to motivate teams and individuals to continue to innovate. Organizations can recognize and reward innovation by celebrating successes, acknowledging the contributions of team members, and providing incentives for innovative ideas and solutions.

6: Providing Resources and Support

To encourage innovation in teams, organizations need to provide teams with the resources and support they need to be successful. This can include access to training and development opportunities, funding for innovation projects, and support from leadership.

7: Encouraging a Growth Mindset

A growth mindset is essential for encouraging innovation in teams, as it promotes the belief that abilities can be developed through dedication and hard work. Organizations can encourage a growth mindset by promoting a culture of learning and development, encouraging individuals to embrace challenges and learn from failure.

8: Conclusion

Encouraging innovation in teams requires a combination of factors, including building diverse teams, fostering a culture of psychological safety, providing opportunities for collaboration, encouraging experimentation and risk-taking, recognizing and rewarding innovation, providing resources and support, and encouraging a growth mindset. By cultivating these elements, organizations can harness the collective creativity and expertise of their teams to drive innovation and achieve success.

C: Leading Innovation: The Role of Leaders in Driving Innovation

Leaders play a crucial role in driving innovation within organizations. In this chapter, we will explore the role of leaders in fostering a culture of innovation, supporting innovative initiatives, and leading by example to inspire others to innovate.

1: Setting a Clear Vision and Strategy

Leaders are responsible for setting a clear vision and strategy for innovation within their organizations. This involves defining goals and objectives, outlining priorities, and aligning innovation efforts with the overall strategic direction of the organization.

2: Creating a Culture of Innovation

Leaders are also responsible for creating a culture that values and encourages innovation. This involves promoting open communication, encouraging experimentation and risk-taking, and fostering a climate of psychological safety where employees feel comfortable sharing ideas and taking creative risks.

3: Providing Resources and Support

Leaders play a critical role in providing the resources and support needed to drive innovation. This includes allocating budget and resources to innovation projects, providing access to training and development opportunities, and removing barriers that may hinder innovation efforts.

4: Empowering Employees

Leaders can empower employees to innovate by giving them the autonomy and freedom to explore new ideas and solutions. This involves trusting employees to take ownership of their work, providing them with the tools and resources they need to be successful, and recognizing and rewarding their contributions to innovation.

5: Leading by Example

Leaders can also lead by example to inspire others to innovate. This involves demonstrating a commitment to innovation through their actions and behaviors, such as being open to new ideas, taking risks, and embracing change.

6: Supporting Innovative Initiatives

Leaders play a crucial role in supporting innovative initiatives within their organizations. This involves providing guidance and direction, removing obstacles that may hinder progress, and ensuring that innovative projects are aligned with the organization's strategic goals and objectives.

7: Celebrating Successes and Learning from Failure

Leaders can foster a culture of innovation by celebrating successes and learning from failure. This involves recognizing and rewarding innovative ideas and initiatives that have been successful, as well as encouraging a mindset of continuous learning and improvement.

8: Conclusion

Leaders play a critical role in driving innovation within organizations. By setting a clear vision and strategy, creating a culture of innovation, providing resources and support, empowering employees, leading by example, supporting innovative initiatives, and celebrating successes, leaders can create an environment where innovation thrives and organizations can achieve sustainable growth and success.

Chapter 7
Analytical Tools for Innovation

A: SWOT Analysis

SWOT analysis is a strategic planning tool used to identify and understand an organization's strengths, weaknesses, opportunities, and threats. In this chapter, we will explore how SWOT analysis can be used to inform strategic decision-making and drive organizational success.

1: Understanding SWOT Analysis

SWOT analysis is a simple yet powerful tool that helps organizations gain insights into their internal and external environments. It involves identifying and evaluating internal strengths and weaknesses, as well as external opportunities and threats.

(i): Strengths:

Internal factors that give an organization a competitive advantage, such as a strong brand, skilled workforce, or innovative products.

(ii): Weaknesses:

Internal factors that may hinder an organization's performance, such as outdated technology, poor management, or lack of resources.

(iii): Opportunities:

External factors that could benefit an organization, such as emerging markets, technological advancements, or changing consumer trends.

(iv): Threats:

External factors that could pose a risk to an organization, such as competition, economic downturns, or regulatory changes.

2: Conducting a SWOT Analysis

To conduct a SWOT analysis, organizations can follow these steps:

(i): Identify Strengths:

Evaluate what the organization does well and what sets it apart from competitors. This could include factors such as a strong brand reputation, unique products or services, or a loyal customer base.

(ii): Identify Weaknesses:

Assess areas where the organization may be lacking or could improve. This could include factors such as outdated technology, high employee turnover, or poor financial management.

(iii): Identify Opportunities:

Look for external factors that could benefit the organization. This could include factors such as new market trends, advances in technology, or changes in consumer behavior.

(iv): Identify Threats:

Identify external factors that could pose a risk to the organization. This could include factors such as increased competition, economic downturns, or regulatory changes.

(v): Analyzing and Prioritizing:

Once the SWOT analysis is complete, organizations can analyze the findings and prioritize actions based on the most significant factors identified in each category.

3: Using SWOT Analysis for Strategic Planning

SWOT analysis can be a valuable tool for informing strategic planning and decision-making. By understanding their strengths, weaknesses, opportunities, and threats, organizations can develop strategies to capitalize on their strengths, address their weaknesses, take advantage of opportunities, and mitigate threats.

4: Conclusion

SWOT analysis is a versatile tool that can help organizations gain valuable insights into their internal and external environments. By conducting a thorough SWOT analysis, organizations can make informed decisions, develop effective strategies, and position themselves for long-term success.

B: PESTLE Analysis

PESTLE analysis is a strategic tool used to understand the external environment in which an organization operates. It examines the Political, Economic, Social, Technological, Legal, and Environmental factors that can impact an organization's business operations and decision-making. In this chapter, we will explore how PESTLE analysis can be used to identify key trends and challenges that may affect an organization's strategic planning and decision-making process.

1: Understanding PESTLE Analysis

PESTLE analysis is a framework that helps organizations understand the external factors that can impact their business environment. It provides a comprehensive view of the external forces that may influence an organization's ability to achieve its objectives and strategies.

(i): Political Factors:

These factors relate to the impact of government policies, regulations, and political stability on an organization. Political factors can include government stability, tax policies, trade regulations, and political risk.

(ii): Economic Factors:

Economic factors relate to the broader economic environment in which an organization operates. These factors can include economic growth, inflation rates, exchange rates, and interest rates.

(iii): Social Factors:

Social factors refer to the cultural, demographic, and societal trends that can impact an organization. These factors can include population demographics, lifestyle trends, cultural norms, and social attitudes.

(iv): Technological Factors:

Technological factors relate to the impact of technology on an organization's business operations. These factors can include technological advancements, automation, research and development, and innovation.

(v): Legal Factors:

Legal factors refer to the laws and regulations that can impact an organization's operations. These factors can include employment laws, health and safety regulations, environmental regulations, and industry-specific regulations.

(vi): Environmental Factors:

Environmental factors relate to the impact of environmental issues and sustainability on an organization. These factors can include climate change, environmental regulations, sustainability practices, and corporate social responsibility.

2: Conducting a PESTLE Analysis

To conduct a PESTLE analysis, organizations can follow these steps:

(i): Identify Political Factors:

Evaluate the impact of government policies, regulations, and political stability on the organization.

(ii): Identify Economic Factors:

Assess the broader economic environment, including economic growth, inflation rates, and exchange rates.

(iii): Identify Social Factors:

Consider cultural, demographic, and societal trends that may impact the organization.

(iv): Identify Technological Factors:

Evaluate the impact of technology on the organization's operations and industry.

(v): Identify Legal Factors:

Consider the legal and regulatory environment in which the organization operates.

(vi): Identify Environmental Factors:

Assess the impact of environmental issues and sustainability on the organization.

(vii): Analyzing and Prioritizing:

Once the PESTLE analysis is complete, organizations can analyze the findings and prioritize actions based on the most significant factors identified in each category.

3: Using PESTLE Analysis for Strategic Planning

PESTLE analysis can be a valuable tool for informing strategic planning and decision-making. By understanding the external factors that can impact their business environment, organizations can develop strategies to mitigate risks, capitalize on opportunities, and achieve their objectives.

4: Conclusion

PESTLE analysis is a powerful tool that can help organizations understand the external factors that can impact their business environment. By conducting a thorough PESTLE analysis, organizations can gain valuable insights into the trends and challenges that may affect their strategic planning and decision-making process, allowing them to develop strategies that are well-informed and resilient to external changes.

C: Root Cause Analysis

Root cause analysis (RCA) is a method used to identify the underlying causes of problems or issues within an organization. By understanding the root causes of problems, organizations can develop effective solutions that address the underlying issues, rather than just treating the symptoms. In this chapter, we will explore how root cause analysis works and how it can be used to drive continuous improvement within an organization.

1: Understanding Root Cause Analysis

Root cause analysis is a systematic process for identifying the underlying causes of problems or issues. It involves looking beyond the immediate symptoms of a problem to identify the underlying factors that contributed to the issue. By addressing these root causes, organizations can prevent the problem from recurring in the future.

2: The Process of Root Cause Analysis

The process of root cause analysis typically involves the following steps:

(i): Identify the Problem:

Clearly define the problem or issue that needs to be addressed.

(ii): Gather Data:

Collect relevant data and information related to the problem, including when and where it occurred, who was involved, and any other relevant details.

(iii): Identify Possible Causes:

Brainstorm potential causes of the problem, considering factors such as human error, equipment failure, process issues, or external factors.

(iv): Narrow Down the Causes:

Evaluate the potential causes to determine which ones are most likely to be the root causes of the problem.

(v): Identify the Root Cause:

Conduct further analysis, such as using tools like the "5 Whys" or fishbone diagrams, to identify the root cause or causes of the problem.

(vi): Develop Solutions:

Once the root cause has been identified, develop and implement solutions that address the underlying issues.

(vii): Monitor and Evaluate:

Monitor the effectiveness of the solutions and evaluate whether they have successfully addressed the root cause of the problem.

3: Benefits of Root Cause Analysis

Root cause analysis offers several benefits for organizations, including:

(i): Preventing Recurrence:

By addressing the root causes of problems, organizations can prevent them from recurring in the future.

(ii): Continuous Improvement:

Root cause analysis helps organizations identify areas for improvement and drive continuous improvement initiatives.

(iii): Cost Savings:

By addressing the root causes of problems, organizations can reduce costs associated with recurring issues and downtime.

4: Using Root Cause Analysis for Continuous Improvement

Root cause analysis is a valuable tool for driving continuous improvement within an organization. By systematically identifying and addressing the underlying causes of problems, organizations can improve their processes, increase efficiency, and enhance overall performance.

5: Conclusion

Root cause analysis is a powerful tool for identifying and addressing the underlying causes of problems within an organization. By using root cause analysis to drive continuous improvement, organizations can enhance their processes, reduce costs, and achieve better outcomes.

D: Design Thinking

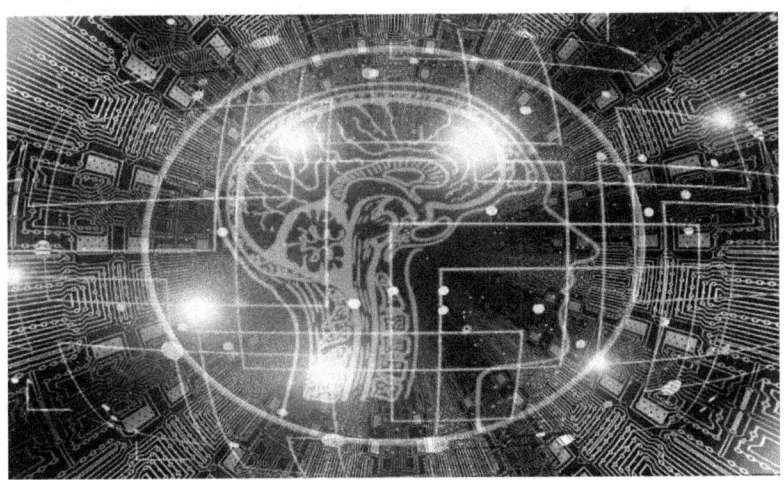

Design thinking is a human-centered approach to innovation that focuses on understanding the needs of users, challenging assumptions, and redefining problems to identify innovative solutions. In this chapter, we will explore the principles of design thinking and how it can be applied to drive innovation and solve complex problems.

1: Understanding Design Thinking

Design thinking is a problem-solving methodology that emphasizes empathy, experimentation, and collaboration. It is a non-linear, iterative process that seeks to understand the user's needs, challenge assumptions, and redefine problems in order to identify innovative solutions.

2: The Design Thinking Process

The design thinking process typically consists of five key stages:

(i): Empathize:

The first stage of the process involves empathizing with the user to understand their needs, motivations, and challenges. This often involves conducting interviews, observations, and surveys to gain insights into the user's perspective.

(ii): Define:

The define stage involves defining the problem statement based on insights gathered during the empathize stage. This involves synthesizing information, identifying patterns, and reframing the problem to ensure it is well-defined and focused.

(iii): Ideate:

In the ideate stage, teams brainstorm a wide range of possible solutions to the defined problem. This involves generating as many ideas as possible without judgment and building on each other's ideas to explore new possibilities.

(iv): Prototype:

The prototype stage involves creating tangible representations of the ideas generated during the ideate stage. Prototypes can take many forms, from sketches and mockups to physical models and digital prototypes.

(v): Test:

The final stage of the process involves testing the prototypes with users to gather feedback and insights. This feedback is used to refine the prototypes and iterate on the design until a viable solution is developed.

3: Key Principles of Design Thinking

Design thinking is guided by several key principles, including:

(i): Human-Centered:

Design thinking puts the needs of users at the center of the process, ensuring that solutions are relevant and meaningful to those who will use them.

(ii): Iterative:

Design thinking is an iterative process, with teams revisiting and refining their ideas based on feedback and insights gathered throughout the process.

(iii): Collaborative:

Design thinking encourages collaboration and multidisciplinary teamwork, bringing together individuals with diverse skills and perspectives to solve complex problems.

(iv): Experimental:

Design thinking embraces experimentation and encourages teams to take risks and explore new ideas without fear of failure.

4: Applying Design Thinking to Innovation

Design thinking can be applied to drive innovation in a wide range of contexts, from product design and development to process improvement and organizational change. By focusing on understanding user needs, challenging assumptions, and redefining problems, design thinking can help organizations develop innovative solutions that address real-world challenges.

5: Conclusion

Design thinking is a powerful approach to innovation that can help organizations develop innovative solutions to complex problems. By focusing on empathy, experimentation, and collaboration, design thinking can help organizations drive meaningful change and achieve better outcomes for users and stakeholders.

Chapter 8
The Future of Analytical Thinking And Innovation

A: Trends Shaping Analytical Thinking and Innovation

Analytical thinking and innovation are constantly evolving to meet the demands of a rapidly changing world. In this chapter, we will explore some of the key trends that are shaping the future of analytical thinking and innovation, and how organizations can adapt to these trends to drive success.

1: Data-Driven Decision Making

One of the most significant trends shaping analytical thinking and innovation is the increasing reliance on data-driven decision-making. Organizations are increasingly using data analytics and business intelligence tools to analyze large volumes of data and derive insights that inform their decision-making processes.

2: Artificial Intelligence and Machine Learning

Artificial intelligence (AI) and machine learning (ML) are also having a profound impact on analytical thinking and innovation. These technologies are enabling organizations to automate tasks, improve predictive analytics, and uncover new insights from data that were previously impossible to obtain.

3: Agile and Lean Approaches to Innovation

Agile and lean approaches to innovation are becoming increasingly popular as organizations seek to accelerate their innovation processes and respond quickly to changing market conditions. These approaches emphasize rapid iteration, customer feedback, and continuous improvement.

4: Design Thinking and Human-Centered Design

Design thinking and human-centered design are also playing a significant role in shaping analytical thinking and innovation. These approaches emphasize understanding the needs of users, challenging assumptions, and redefining problems to identify innovative solutions.

5: Cross-Disciplinary Collaboration

Another trend shaping analytical thinking and innovation is the increasing emphasis on cross-disciplinary collaboration. Organizations are recognizing the value of bringing together individuals with diverse skills and perspectives to solve complex problems and drive innovation.

6: Sustainability and Corporate Social Responsibility

Sustainability and corporate social responsibility (CSR) are also influencing analytical thinking and innovation. Organizations are increasingly focused on developing sustainable business practices and products that have a positive impact on society and the environment.

7: Conclusion

Analytical thinking and innovation are evolving rapidly, driven by trends such as data-driven decision-making, AI and ML, agile and lean approaches, design thinking, cross-disciplinary collaboration, and sustainability. By embracing these trends and adapting their approaches to innovation, organizations can drive meaningful change and achieve long-term success in a rapidly changing world.

B: The Impact of Technology on Innovation

Technology plays a crucial role in driving innovation, enabling organizations to develop new products, services, and processes that transform industries and drive economic growth. In this chapter, we will explore the impact of technology on innovation and how organizations can leverage technology to drive innovation in their own operations.

1: Accelerating the Pace of Innovation

Technology has dramatically accelerated the pace of innovation, allowing organizations to develop and bring new products and services to market faster than ever before. Advances in areas such as artificial intelligence, robotics, and automation have enabled organizations to streamline their operations and develop innovative solutions more quickly and efficiently.

2: Enabling Remote Collaboration

Technology has also transformed how organizations collaborate and innovate. With the rise of digital collaboration tools, teams can now work together from anywhere in the world, enabling more diverse and cross-disciplinary teams to come together and drive innovation.

3: Empowering Data-Driven Decision Making

One of the most significant impacts of technology on innovation is the ability to collect, analyze, and leverage data to drive decision-making. Organizations can now use data analytics and business intelligence tools to gain insights into customer behavior, market trends, and operational performance, enabling them to make more informed decisions and drive innovation.

4: Fostering a Culture of Experimentation

Technology has also fostered a culture of experimentation within organizations, enabling them to test new ideas and concepts quickly and at a lower cost. Technologies such as cloud computing and rapid prototyping tools have made it easier for organizations to experiment and iterate on ideas, leading to more innovative solutions.

5: Enhancing Customer Engagement

Technology has also transformed how organizations engage with their customers, enabling more personalized and interactive experiences. Through digital channels such as social media, organizations can gather feedback, understand customer needs, and tailor their products and services to meet those needs more effectively.

6: Conclusion

Technology has had a profound impact on innovation, accelerating the pace of change, enabling remote collaboration, empowering data-driven decision-making, fostering a culture of experimentation, and enhancing customer engagement. By embracing technology and leveraging it effectively, organizations can drive innovation, stay competitive, and achieve long-term success in today's rapidly evolving business landscape.

C: Developing Future-Ready Analytical Skills

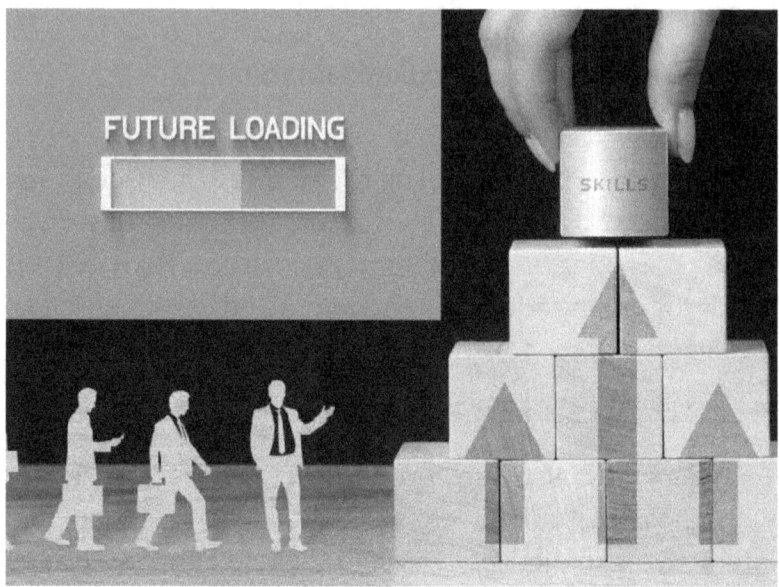

In today's rapidly evolving business landscape, having strong analytical skills is more important than ever. In this chapter, we will explore the key analytical skills that are essential for success in the future and how individuals can develop these skills to stay competitive in their careers.

1: Critical Thinking

Critical thinking is a fundamental analytical skill that involves objectively analyzing and evaluating information to make informed decisions. To develop critical thinking skills, individuals can practice asking probing questions, considering alternative perspectives, and evaluating the credibility of sources.

2: Data Analysis

Data analysis involves interpreting and making sense of data to uncover insights and inform decision-making. To develop data analysis skills, individuals can learn statistical techniques, data visualization tools, and data manipulation techniques.

3: Problem-Solving

Problem-solving is another key analytical skill that involves identifying, analyzing, and solving problems effectively. To develop problem-solving skills, individuals can practice breaking down complex problems into smaller, manageable parts, identifying possible solutions, and evaluating the effectiveness of those solutions.

4: Decision-Making

Decision-making involves making choices based on a thorough analysis of available information and considering the potential outcomes. To develop decision-making skills, individuals can practice weighing the pros and cons of different options, considering the long-term implications of their decisions, and seeking feedback from others.

5: Creativity and Innovation

Creativity and innovation are essential for developing novel solutions to complex problems. To develop creativity and innovation skills, individuals can practice brainstorming ideas, challenging assumptions, and exploring new ways of thinking.

6: Communication

Communication is a critical skill for conveying complex ideas and insights to others. To develop communication skills, individuals can practice presenting information clearly and concisely, tailoring their message to their audience, and listening actively to others.

7: Adaptability

Adaptability is essential in today's fast-paced business environment, where change is constant. To develop adaptability skills, individuals can practice staying open to new ideas and ways of working, seeking out new learning opportunities, and embracing change as an opportunity for growth.

8: Conclusion

Developing future-ready analytical skills is essential for success in today's dynamic business environment. By focusing on developing critical thinking, data analysis, problem-solving, decision-making, creativity, innovation, communication, and adaptability skills, individuals can position themselves for success and stay competitive in their careers.

Chapter 9
Case Studies in Analytical Thinking and Innovation

A: Real-World Examples of Analytical Thinking and Innovation

In this chapter, we will explore real-world examples of how organizations have used analytical thinking and innovation to solve complex problems, drive growth, and achieve success. These examples demonstrate the practical application of analytical thinking and innovation in a variety of industries and contexts.

1: Netflix: Personalized Recommendation Algorithm

Netflix is a prime example of how analytical thinking and innovation can transform an industry. Netflix uses a sophisticated recommendation algorithm to personalize content recommendations for its users based on their viewing history, preferences, and behavior. This algorithm has helped Netflix increase user engagement and retention, driving its success as a leading streaming service.

2: Tesla: Electric Vehicles and Autopilot

Tesla has revolutionized the automotive industry with its electric vehicles and advanced autopilot technology. Tesla's use of analytical thinking and innovation has enabled it to develop cutting-edge electric vehicles that offer superior performance and range compared to traditional gasoline-powered cars. Tesla's autopilot technology also demonstrates its commitment to innovation, paving the way for autonomous driving in the future.

3: Amazon: Supply Chain Optimization

Amazon is known for its efficient supply chain management, which is driven by analytical thinking and innovation. Amazon uses advanced analytics and machine learning algorithms to optimize its supply chain, ensuring that products are delivered to customers quickly and efficiently. This has helped Amazon become the world's largest online retailer, with a reputation for fast and reliable delivery.

4: Google: Search Engine and AI

Google's search engine is a testament to the power of analytical thinking and innovation. Google's search algorithm uses complex algorithms to deliver relevant search results to users, making it the most popular search engine in the world. Google has also been a pioneer in artificial intelligence (AI), developing technologies such as Google Assistant and Google Duplex that demonstrate the potential of AI to transform how we interact with technology.

5: Airbnb: Disrupting the Hospitality Industry

Airbnb has disrupted the hospitality industry by using analytical thinking and innovation to create a platform that connects travelers with unique accommodations around the world. Airbnb's platform uses data analytics to match travelers with accommodations that meet their preferences, enabling them to have unique and personalized travel experiences.

6: Conclusion

These examples demonstrate how organizations can use analytical thinking and innovation to drive success and disrupt industries. By leveraging data, technology, and creative thinking, organizations can solve complex problems, drive growth, and stay competitive in today's fast-paced business environment.

B: Lessons Learned from Successful Innovators

In this chapter, we will explore the key lessons that can be learned from successful innovators who have achieved remarkable success through their innovative approaches and thinking.

1: Think Outside the Box

Successful innovators are not afraid to think outside the box and challenge the status quo. They are willing to explore unconventional ideas and approaches, which often leads to breakthrough innovations that disrupt industries and create new markets.

2: Embrace Failure as a Learning Opportunity

Failure is an inevitable part of the innovation process, but successful innovators embrace failure as a learning opportunity. They understand that failure is not a sign of weakness, but rather a necessary step on the path to success. By learning from their failures, innovators are able to iterate and improve their ideas, ultimately leading to success.

3: Focus on the User

Successful innovators understand the importance of focusing on the user and designing products and services that meet their needs. By putting the user at the center of their innovation process, innovators are able to create products and services that resonate with their target audience and drive adoption.

4: Stay Agile and Adaptable

The business landscape is constantly evolving, and successful innovators are able to stay agile and adaptable in the face of change. They are able to pivot quickly in response to changing market conditions and customer needs, allowing them to stay ahead of the competition.

5: Foster a Culture of Innovation

Successful innovators understand that innovation is a team effort, and they foster a culture of innovation within their organizations. They encourage creativity and experimentation, and they provide the support and resources needed for their teams to innovate and succeed.

6: Continuously Learn and Grow

Innovation is a journey, not a destination, and successful innovators are continuously learning and growing. They seek out new ideas and perspectives, and they are always looking for ways to improve and innovate.

7: Conclusion

By embracing these key lessons from successful innovators, individuals and organizations can cultivate a mindset of innovation and drive success in today's rapidly changing business landscape.

Chapter 10
Putting It All Together: A Roadmap to Analytical Thinking and Innovation

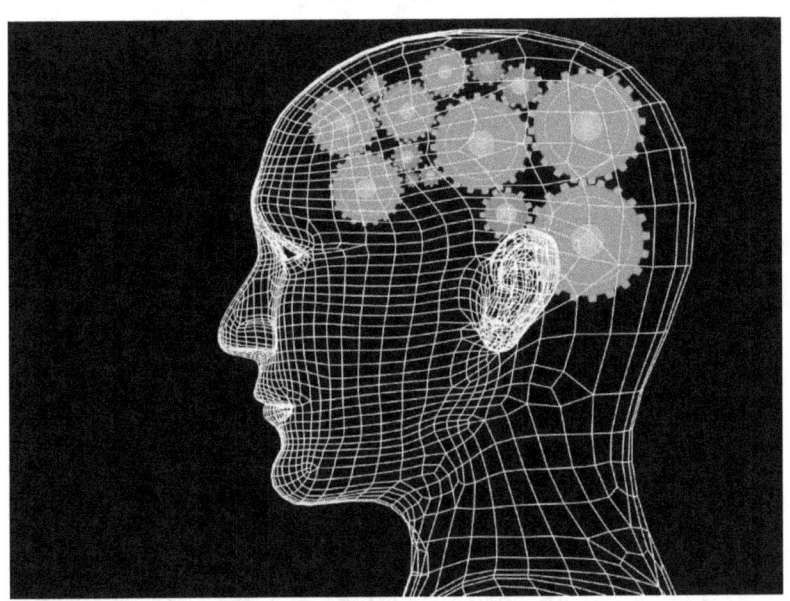

A: Summary of Key Concepts

In this chapter, we will summarize the key concepts covered in this book on analytical thinking and innovation. These concepts provide a framework for understanding how analytical thinking and innovation can drive success in today's business environment.

1: Analytical Thinking

Analytical thinking is a critical skill that involves breaking down complex problems into smaller, more manageable parts and analyzing them systematically to identify patterns, trends, and insights. It involves the use of logic, reasoning, and data analysis to make informed decisions and solve problems effectively.

2: Innovation

Innovation is the process of creating new ideas, products, or services that add value to customers or solve a problem in a new way. It involves creativity, experimentation, and a willingness to take risks to develop new and innovative solutions.

3: The Relationship Between Analytical Thinking and Innovation

Analytical thinking and innovation are closely related, as analytical thinking provides the foundation for identifying opportunities for innovation and developing innovative solutions. Analytical thinking helps to ensure that innovations are based on sound reasoning and analysis, increasing their chances of success.

4: Key Skills for Analytical Thinking and Innovation

Some key skills for analytical thinking and innovation include critical thinking, data analysis, problem-solving, creativity, and adaptability. These skills are essential for identifying opportunities for innovation, developing innovative solutions, and driving success in today's business environment.

5: Trends Shaping Analytical Thinking and Innovation

Several trends are shaping the future of analytical thinking and innovation, including data-driven decision-making, artificial intelligence and machine learning, agile and lean approaches to innovation, design thinking, cross-disciplinary collaboration, and sustainability. By embracing these trends, organizations can drive innovation and stay competitive in today's rapidly changing business landscape.

6: Lessons Learned from Successful Innovators

Successful innovators have several key traits and practices in common, including thinking outside the box, embracing failure as a learning opportunity, focusing on the user, staying agile and adaptable, fostering a culture of innovation, and continuously learning and growing. By adopting these traits and practices, individuals and organizations can drive success through innovation.

7: Conclusion

Analytical thinking and innovation are critical for driving success in today's business environment. By developing strong analytical thinking skills, fostering a culture of innovation, and embracing key trends and lessons from successful innovators, individuals and organizations can drive innovation, solve complex problems, and achieve success in today's rapidly changing world.

B: Practical Tips for Enhancing Analytical Thinking and Innovation

In this chapter, we will provide practical tips for enhancing analytical thinking and fostering innovation. These tips are designed to help individuals and organizations develop the skills and mindset needed to drive innovation and solve complex problems effectively.

1: Develop a Curious Mindset

Curiosity is a key driver of innovation. Stay curious about the world around you, ask questions, and seek out new ideas and perspectives. This can help you uncover new opportunities for innovation and develop creative solutions to problems.

2: Practice Critical Thinking

Critical thinking is essential for analytical thinking and innovation. Practice analyzing information, questioning assumptions, and evaluating arguments to strengthen your critical thinking skills. This will help you make informed decisions and solve problems more effectively.

3: Embrace Failure as a Learning Opportunity

Failure is a natural part of the innovation process. Instead of fearing failure, embrace it as an opportunity to learn and grow. Analyze what went wrong, identify lessons learned, and use this knowledge to improve your future innovation efforts.

4: Collaborate with Others

Collaboration is key to successful innovation. Work with colleagues, partners, and customers to generate new ideas, gain diverse perspectives, and develop innovative solutions. Collaborative environments foster creativity and can lead to breakthrough innovations.

5: Use Data to Inform Decision-Making

Data can provide valuable insights that can inform your innovation efforts. Use data analytics tools to analyze data, identify trends, and uncover patterns that can guide your decision-making process. Data-driven decision-making can lead to more effective and successful innovation.

6: Experiment and Iterate

Innovation is an iterative process. Don't be afraid to experiment with new ideas and approaches, and be willing to iterate on your solutions based on feedback and results. This iterative approach can help you refine your ideas and develop more innovative solutions over time.

7: Foster a Culture of Innovation

Create a work environment that encourages and supports innovation. Encourage employees to share ideas, experiment with new approaches, and take risks. Recognize and reward innovative thinking to reinforce a culture of innovation within your organization.

8: Stay Agile and Adaptable

The business landscape is constantly evolving, so it's important to stay agile and adaptable in your approach to innovation. Be willing to pivot quickly in response to changing market conditions and customer needs, and be open to new ideas and ways of working.

9: Conclusion

By following these practical tips, individuals and organizations can enhance their analytical thinking skills, foster a culture of innovation, and drive success in today's dynamic business environment. By embracing curiosity, practicing critical thinking, collaborating with others, using data to inform decision-making, experimenting and iterating, fostering a culture of innovation, and staying agile and adaptable, you can enhance your analytical thinking and innovation capabilities and achieve success in your innovation efforts.

C: Personal Action Plan for Continued Growth in Analytical Thinking and Innovation

In this chapter, we will outline a personal action plan for individuals looking to enhance their analytical thinking and foster innovation. This action plan includes practical steps and strategies that individuals can take to develop their analytical thinking skills, drive innovation, and achieve success in their personal and professional lives.

1: Assess Your Current Skills and Mindset

Begin by assessing your current analytical thinking skills and mindset. Reflect on your strengths and areas for improvement, and identify any barriers or challenges that may be hindering your ability to think analytically and innovate.

2: Set Clear Goals

Set clear, achievable goals for enhancing your analytical thinking and fostering innovation. Your goals should be specific, measurable, attainable, relevant, and time-bound (SMART). For example, you could set a goal to learn a new data analysis technique within the next three months.

3: Develop a Learning Plan

Develop a learning plan to help you achieve your goals. This plan should include specific actions you will take to enhance your analytical thinking skills and foster innovation, such as taking online courses, attending workshops, or reading books on the subject.

4: Practice Regularly

Practice is key to improving your analytical thinking skills and fostering innovation. Look for opportunities to practice your skills in your daily life, such as by solving puzzles, analyzing data, or brainstorming ideas for new projects.

5: Seek Feedback and Learn from Others

Seek feedback from others to help you improve your analytical thinking skills and foster innovation. This could include seeking input from colleagues, mentors, or experts in your field. Learn from their experiences and insights to enhance your own skills and knowledge.

6: Experiment with New Ideas

Be willing to experiment with new ideas and approaches to problem-solving. Don't be afraid to take risks or try new things, as this can lead to breakthrough innovations and new opportunities for growth.

7: Reflect on Your Progress

Regularly reflect on your progress towards your goals and adjust your action plan as needed. Celebrate your successes and learn from any setbacks or challenges you encounter along the way.

8: Conclusion

By following this personal action plan, you can enhance your analytical thinking skills, foster innovation, and achieve success in your personal and professional life. By setting clear goals, developing a learning plan, practicing regularly, seeking feedback, experimenting with new ideas, and reflecting on your progress, you can continue to grow and develop as an analytical thinker and innovator.

Conclusion

Embracing Analytical Thinking and Innovation for a Brighter Future

A: Final Thoughts on the Power of Analytical Thinking and Innovation

In this final chapter, we will reflect on the power of analytical thinking and innovation and how they can drive success and create positive change in both personal and professional settings.

1: The Impact of Analytical Thinking

Analytical thinking is a powerful tool that can help individuals and organizations solve complex problems, make informed decisions, and drive innovation. By breaking down problems into smaller, more manageable parts and analyzing them systematically, analytical thinking can lead to more effective solutions and better outcomes.

2: The Role of Innovation

Innovation is the driving force behind progress and growth. It is through innovation that new ideas are developed, new products and services are created, and new markets are discovered. Innovation is essential for staying competitive in today's fast-paced business environment and for driving positive change in society.

3: The Intersection of Analytical Thinking and Innovation

The intersection of analytical thinking and innovation is where the magic happens. By combining the analytical skills needed to understand complex problems with the creative thinking needed to develop innovative solutions, individuals and organizations can achieve remarkable results.

4: Embracing a Mindset of Continuous Improvement

To harness the power of analytical thinking and innovation, individuals and organizations must embrace a mindset of continuous improvement. This means constantly seeking out new ideas, experimenting with new approaches, and learning from both successes and failures.

5: Conclusion

Analytical thinking and innovation are not just skills; they are mindsets that can drive success and create positive change. By developing strong analytical thinking skills, fostering a culture of innovation, and embracing new ideas and approaches, individuals and organizations can achieve their goals, solve complex problems, and make a meaningful impact in the world.

6: Final Words

As we conclude this exploration of analytical thinking and innovation, I encourage you to continue developing your analytical thinking skills, fostering innovation, and embracing change. By doing so, you can unlock your full potential and make a lasting impact in your personal and professional life.

B: Encouragement for Readers to Apply Concepts in Their Lives

In this chapter, we will provide encouragement for readers to apply the concepts of analytical thinking and innovation in their personal and professional lives. We will discuss the benefits of applying these concepts and provide practical tips for getting started.

1: Benefits of Applying Analytical Thinking and Innovation

Applying analytical thinking and innovation can have numerous benefits, including:

(i): Improved Problem-Solving:

Analytical thinking can help you break down complex problems into smaller, more manageable parts, making them easier to solve.

(ii): Enhanced Decision-Making:

Analytical thinking can help you make more informed decisions by analyzing data and information more effectively.

(iii): Increased Creativity:

Innovation can help you develop creative solutions to problems and come up with new ideas.

(iv): Career Advancement:

Applying these concepts can help you stand out in your career by demonstrating your ability to think critically and innovate.

(v): Personal Growth:

Applying these concepts can help you develop valuable skills that can benefit you in all areas of your life.

2: Practical Tips for Applying Analytical Thinking and Innovation

To apply these concepts in your life, consider the following tips:

(i): Start Small:

Begin by applying these concepts to small, everyday problems to build your skills and confidence.

(ii): Seek Feedback:

Ask for feedback from others to help you improve your analytical thinking and innovative skills.

(iii): Learn Continuously:

Stay curious and keep learning new things to enhance your analytical thinking and innovative abilities.

(iv): Collaborate with Others:

Work with others to brainstorm ideas and develop innovative solutions to problems.

(v): Stay Positive:

Embrace failure as a learning opportunity and stay positive as you apply these concepts in your life.

3: Conclusion

By applying the concepts of analytical thinking and innovation in your personal and professional life, you can enhance your problem-solving abilities, make more informed decisions, and drive positive change. Start applying these concepts today to unlock your full potential and achieve success in all areas of your life.

Read More Interesting Book!